The Mini Manual of
One Liners

First published by Parragon in 2010

Parragon

Queen Street House

4 Queen Street

Bath BA1 1HE, UK

Copyright © Parragon Books Ltd 2010

Layout by Stonecastle Graphics Ltd

ISBN 978-1-4075-9360-9

Printed in China

The Mini Manual of
One Liners

PaRragon

Bath · New York · Singapore · Hong Kong · Cologne · Delhi · Melbourne

Contents

Introduction

Noah was an amateur;
the *Titanic* was built by professionals.
Malcolm Allison

Brilliant conversation was once (and remains) an art and those with talent (Samuel Johnson, Oscar Wilde, Dorothy Parker to name but a few) have produced some masterpieces of repartee.

The Mini Manual of One Liners contains a variety of snippets ranging from the subtly clever to the outright vitriolic. And not only do we admire alacrity of wit but there is something in human nature that derives great amusement from the verbal slaughtering of one person by another.

Perhaps it is the modern equivalent of watching the Christians thrown to the lions. This collection of wicked understatement and acidic oratory should satisfy the most voracious appetite.

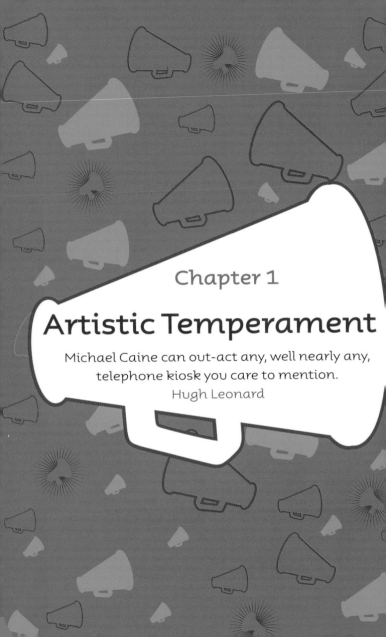

Chapter 1

Artistic Temperament

Michael Caine can out-act any, well nearly any,
telephone kiosk you care to mention.
Hugh Leonard

Stage and screen, music, art and literature—a selection of inventive invective and critical commentary about those in the limelight.

· · · · · ·

He looks like a half-melted rubber bulldog.
John Simon (of Walter Matthau)

· · · · · ·

The Henry Fondas lay on the evening
like a damp mackintosh.
Noël Coward

· · · · · ·

Audrey Hepburn is a walking X-ray.
Billy Wilder

· · · · · ·

Wet, she was a star—dry she ain't.
Joe Pasternak (of swimmer turned actress
Esther Williams)

Talk low, talk slow, and don't say too much.
John Wayne

• • • • •

Tallulah Bankhead barged down the Nile last night as Cleopatra—and sank.
John Mason Brown

• • • • •

His features resemble a fossilized washrag.
Alan Brien (of Steve McQueen)

• • • • •

Every great work of art has two faces, one toward its own time and one toward the future, toward eternity.
Daniel Barenboim

• • • • •

Madonna's so hairy—when she lifted her arm I thought it was Tina Turner in her armpit.
Joan Rivers

She has only two things going for her—a father and a mother.
John Simon (of Liza Minnelli)

• • • • •

I always try to balance the light with the heavy—a few tears of human spirit in with the sequins and the fringes.
Bette Midler

• • • • •

If Woody Allen didn't exist, then somebody would have knitted him.
Lesley White

• • • • •

ney shot too many pictures and not enough actors.
Walter Winchell

• • • • •

When I grow up, I still want to be a director.
Steven Spielberg

Editing the film *The Boy Friend*, a gorilla in boxing gloves wielding a pair of garden shears could have done a better job.
Ken Russell

• • • • •

Getting the costumes right in *Cleopatra* was like polishing the fish-knives on the *Titanic*.
Julian Barnes

• • • • •

Pardon me Ma'am, I thought you were a guy I knew in Pittsburgh.
Groucho Marx (to Greta Garbo in *Bring on the Empty Horses*)

• • • • •

James Cagney rolled through the film like a very belligerent barrel.
Noël Coward

• • • • •

Ryan O'Neal is so stiff and clumsy he can't even act a part requiring him to be stiff and clumsy
Jay Cocks

The best time I ever had with Joan (Crawford) was when I pushed her down the stairs in *Whatever Happened to Baby Jane*.
Bette Davis

• • • • •

Say anything you want about me, but you make fun of my picture and you'll regret it the rest of your fat midget life.
Joshua Logan (to Truman Capote)

• • • • •

This is one of those films that should never have been released—not even on parole.
Christopher Tookey

• • • • •

Nowadays Mitchum doesn't so much act as point his suit at people.
Russell Davies

• • • • •

Book: what they make a movie out of for television.
Leonard Louis Levinson

To suggest that *Break A Leg* needs a splint would
be to offer it an unjustifiable hope of recovery.
Clive Barnes

•••••

Cher looked like a bag of tattooed bones
in a sequined slingshot.
Worst Dressed List

•••••

Marilyn Monroe was good at playing abstract
confusion in the same way that a midget
is good at being short.
Clive James

•••••

He directed rehearsals with all the
airy deftness of a rheumatic deacon producing
Macbeth for a church social.
Noël Coward (of J.R. Crawford)

•••••

This film wasn't released—it escaped.
James Caan

Never judge a book by its movie.
J.W. Eagan

• • • • •

Television is chewing gum for the mind.
Frank Lloyd Wright

• • • • •

It's the movies that have really been running
things in America ever since they were
invented—they show you what to do, how to
do it, when to do it, how to feel about it,
and how to look how you feel about it.
Andy Warhol

• • • • •

think that first nights should come near the end
of a play's run—as indeed they often do.
Peter Ustinov

• • • • •

Television: an electric device which, when
turned off, stimulates conversation.
Anon

You never get a chance to sit down
unless you're a king.
Josephine Hull (on acting in Shakespeare's plays

• • • • •

I suppose I could make changes in my play but
who am I to tamper with a masterpiece.
Oscar Wilde

• • • • •

The Blaises were both a bit desiccated and lacke
vitality to such a degree that one felt oxygen
should be served after the fish.
Noël Coward

• • • • •

It was one of those plays in which all the actor
unfortunately enunciated very clearly.
Robert Benchley

• • • • •

The embarrassing thing is that the salad dressi
is outgrossing my films.
Paul Newman

An artist is someone who produces things that people don't need to have but that he—for some reason—thinks it would be a good idea to give them.
Andy Warhol

. . . . .

It's about as long as *Parsifal*, and not as funny.
Noël Coward (on *Camelot*)

. . . . .

He's miscast and she's Miss Taylor.
Emlyn Williams (of Burton and Taylor in *Private Lives*)

. . . . .

I've seen Don entertain fifty times and I've always enjoyed his joke.
Johnny Carson

. . . . .

I don't have big anxieties—I wish I did, I'd be much more interesting.
Roy Lichtenstein

The press was almost unanimous on one thing, and that was that I should never have been allowed to appear in it.
Noël Coward (of his role in *London Calling*)

• • • • •

The press is easier squashed than squared.
Winston Churchill

• • • • •

A critic is a man who knows the way but can't drive the car.
Kenneth Tynan

• • • • •

A censor is a man who knows more than he thinks you ought to.
Laurence J. Peter

• • • • •

It's the gossip columnist's business to write about what is none of his business.
Louis Kronenberger

The secret to film is that it's an illusion.
George Lucas

• • • • •

No self-respecting fish would be wrapped
in a Murdoch newspaper.
Mike Royko

• • • • •

You should always believe all you read
in the newspapers, as this makes
them more interesting.
Rose Macaulay

• • • • •

Journalism is unreadable,
and literature is not read.
Oscar Wilde

• • • • •

Once a newspaper touches a story the facts are
lost for ever, even to the protagonists.
Norman Mailer

Rock journalism is people who can't write
interviewing people who can't talk for
people who can't read.
Frank Zappa

· · · · ·

Only the names have been changed,
to protect the guilty.
Noël Coward (of his short story
What Mad Pursuit)

· · · · ·

Your manuscript is both good and original; but
the part that is good is not original, and the part
that is original is not good.
Samuel Johnson

· · · · ·

This book fills a much needed gap.
Moses Hadas

· · · · ·

It was very intelligent and absolute rubbish.
Noël Coward (of a book written
about his plays)

Art for art's sake is a philosophy
of the well-fed.
Frank Lloyd Wright

• • • • •

He is able to turn an unplotted, unworkable
manuscript into an unplotted and unworkable
manuscript with a lot of sex.
Tom Volpe (of Harold Robbins)

• • • • •

The work of a queasy undergraduate
scratching his pimples.
Virginia Woolf (of James Joyce)

• • • • •

A louse in the locks of literature.
Alfred, Lord Tennyson (of a critic)

• • • • •

I regard this novel as a work without
any redeeming social value, unless it can
be recycled as a cardboard box.
Ellen Goodman (of Danielle Steel's
novel, Message from Nam)

Classic: a book which people praise
and don't read.
Samuel Johnson

Mark Twain

• • • • •

I never read a book before reviewing it;
it prejudices a man so.
Sydney Smith

• • • • •

A writer of dictionaries, a harmless drudge.
Samuel Johnson

• • • • •

The way Bernard Shaw believes in himself is
very refreshing in these atheistic days when
so many people believe in no God at all.
Israel Zangwill

• • • • •

Henry James was one of the nicest
old ladies I ever met.
William Faulkner

No one but a blockhead ever wrote,
except for money.
Samuel Johnson

• • • • •

I don't want life to imitate
art—I want life to be art.
Carrie Fisher

• • • • •

Discretion is not the better part of biography.
Lytton Strachey

• • • • •

In America only the successful writer is
important, in France all writers are important, in
England no writer is important, and in Australia
you have to explain what a writer is.
Geoffrey Cottrell

• • • • •

When I want to read a novel, I write one.
Benjamin Disraeli

It's amazing how long it takes to complete
something you're not working on.
R.D. Clyde

• • • • •

Always willing to lend a helping hand
to the one above him.
F. Scott Fitzgerald (of Ernest Hemingway)

• • • • •

When Jack Benny plays the violin, it sounds
as though the strings are still in the cat.
Fred Allen

• • • • •

Let's play a medley of your hit!
Oscar Levant (to George Gershwin)

• • • • •

Why do we have all these third-rate foreign
conductors around when we have so many
second-rate ones of our own?
Sir Thomas Beecham

Going to the opera, like getting drunk, is a sin
that carries its own punishment with it.
Hannah More

• • • • •

Too many pieces of music finish too
long after the end.
Igor Stravinsky

• • • • •

azz will endure, as long a people hear it through
their feet instead of their brains.
John Philip Sousa

• • • • •

If one plays good music people don't listen and
if one plays bad music people don't talk.
Oscar Wilde

• • • • •

When Brahms is in extra good spirits,
he sings, *The Grave is My Joy*.
Tchaikovsky

An unalterable and unquestioned law of the musical world requires that the German text of French operas sung by Swedish artists should be translated into Italian for the clearer understanding of English-speaking audiences.
Edith Wharton

• • • • •

He has Van Gogh's ear for music.
Orson Welles (of Donny Osmond)

• • • • •

The mama of Dada.
Clifton Fadiman (of Gertrude Stein)

• • • • •

My art belongs to Dada.
Cole Porter (attrib.)

• • • • •

There are only two styles of portrait painting; the serious and the smirk.
Charles Dickens, *Nicholas Nickleby*, 1839

A Realist is someone who paints what
other people don't paint.
R.J. Richardson

• • • • •

A tortoiseshell cat having a fit in
a platter of tomatoes.
Mark Twain (on a Turner painting)

• • • • •

Every good journalist has a novel in him—which is
an excellent place for it.
Russell Lynes

• • • • •

A journalist has no ideas and the ability
to express them.
Karl Kraus

• • • • •

The English may not like music, but they
absolutely love the noise it makes.
Sir Thomas Beecham

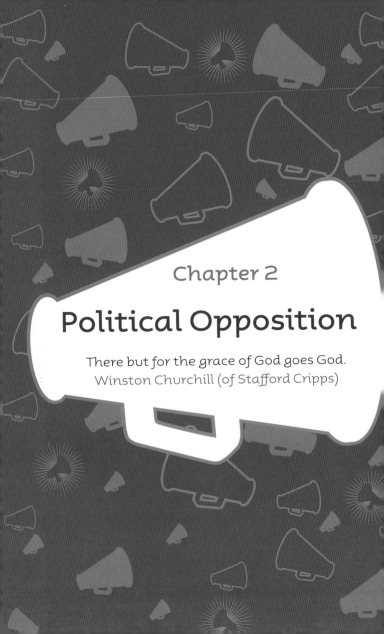

Chapter 2

Political Opposition

There but for the grace of God goes God.
Winston Churchill (of Stafford Cripps)

If politicians must stand up there on their soapboxes, what else can they expect but to be knocked off by a well-aimed witticisim? This section contains a wealth of scornful appraisals of the weaknesses and foibles of those who run the world.

• • • • •

Mr Speaker, I withdraw my statement
that half the cabinet are asses—half
the cabinet are not asses.
Benjamin Disraeli

• • • • •

We all know that Prime Ministers are wedded to
the truth, but like other married couples
they sometimes live apart.
Saki

• • • • •

I think it will be a clash between the political
will and the administrative won't.
Jonathan Lynn and Anthony Jay,
Yes, Prime Minister

The Marxist law of distribution of wealth is
that shortages will be divided equally
among the peasants.
John Guftason

• • • • •

Had he been a much worse man, he would
have done Canada much less harm.
Sir Richard Cartwright (of John A. Macdonald)

• • • • •

He is a self-made man and worships his creator.
Benjamin Disraeli (of John Bright)

• • • • •

If voting changed anything they'd make it illegal.
Anon

• • • • •

A sophistical rhetorician inebriated with the
exuberance of his own verbosity.
Benjamin Disraeli (of William Gladstone)

He is a sheep in sheep's clothing.
Winston Churchill (of Clement Attlee)

• • • • •

It's a recession when your neighbor loses his job;
it's a depression when you lose yours.
Harry S. Truman

• • • • •

In war you don't have to be nice;
you only have to be right.
Winston Churchill

• • • • •

He can compress the most words into the
smallest ideas better than any man I ever met.
Abraham Lincoln

• • • • •

When the eagles are silent, the
parrots begin to jabber.
Winston Churchill

Ronald Reagan is a triumph
of the embalmer's art.
Gore Vidal

• • • • •

There's not a liberal America and a conservative
America—there's the United States of America.
Barack Obama

• • • • •

There is only one thing worse than fighting with
allies, and that is fighting without them.
Winston Churchill

• • • • •

A Byzantine logothete.
Theodore Roosevelt (of Woodrow Wilson)

• • • • •

Sir Stafford has a brilliant mind—until
it is made up.
Violet Bonham Carter (of Stafford Cripps)

If you are not criticized, you may not be doing much.
Donald Rumsfeld

• • • • •

They are not fit to manage a whelk-stall.
Winston Churchill (of the British Labour Party)

• • • • •

Fleas can be taught nearly anything that
a Congressman can.
Mark Twain

• • • • •

If the Republicans will stop telling lies about
the Democrats, we will stop telling the
truth about them.
Adlai Stevenson

• • • • •

It is not enough to have every intelligent person
in the country voting for me—I need a majority.
Adlai Stevenson

Now that I am no longer President, I find that
I do not win every game of golf I play.
George Bush

• • • • •

He always played the game and he always lost it.
Winston Churchill (of Austen Chamberlain)

• • • • •

If Gladstone fell into the Thames, that would be
a misfortune, and if anybody pulled him out,
that would be a calamity.
Benjamin Disraeli

• • • • •

Ronald Reagan doesn't dye his hair,
he's just prematurely orange.
Gerald Ford (attrib.)

• • • • •

The challenge is to practice politics as the art of
making what appears to be impossible, possible
Hillary Clinton

A politician will always be there
when he needs you.
Ian Walsh

• • • • •

Clement Attlee reminds me of a dead fish
before it has had time to stiffen.
George Orwell

• • • • •

He is a man suffering from petrified adolescence.
Aneurin Bevan (of Winston Churchill)

• • • • •

Choosing between Bush, Clinton, and Perot was
like needing clean underwear but being forced to
decide between three dirty pairs.
Michael Dalton Johnson

• • • • •

Politics is the conduct of public affairs for
private advantage.
Ambrose Bierce

Washington couldn't tell a lie, Nixon couldn't tell the truth, and Reagan couldn't tell the difference.
Mort Sahl

• • • • •

The Secret Service is under orders if Bush is shot, to shoot Quayle.
John Kerry

• • • • •

The problem...is that most members of Congress don't pay attention to what's going on.
John McCain

• • • • •

Military intelligence is a contradiction in terms.
Oswald G. Villard

• • • • •

Politics is derived from two words—poly, meaning many, and tics, meaning small blood-sucking insects.
Chris Clayton

A choice between the lesser of two weevils.
S.J. Perelman (of Gerald Ford and Jimmy Carter)

• • • • •

Al Gore is in danger of becoming
all things to no people.
Paul Bograd

• • • • •

He played too much football without a helmet.
Lyndon B. Johnson (of Gerald Ford)

• • • • •

Dan Quayle taught the kids a valuable
lesson: if you don't study you could wind
up as Vice-President.
Jay Leno

• • • • •

I cannot bring myself to vote for a woman
who has been voice-trained to speak to me
as though my dog had just died.
Keith Waterhouse (of Margaret Thatcher)

Chapter 3

Battle of the Sexes

Scratch a lover, and find a foe.
Dorothy Parker

Men v. women, women v. men, marriage, divorce and a healthy batch of put-downs. Romantic entanglements have always provided the aphorist with a rich source of material.

. . . . .

His wife said she wanted an animal fur, so he bought her a donkey jacket.
Anon

. . . . .

I don't like all-in wrestling—if it's all in, why wrestle?
Mae West

. . . . .

If you're afraid of loneliness, don't marry.
Anton Chekhov

. . . . .

Familiarity breeds contempt—and children.
Mark Twain

Ask him the time and he'll tell you how
the watch was made.
Jane Wyman (of ex-husband Ronald Reagan)

• • • • •

Fred Astaire was great, but don't forget that
Ginger Rogers did everything that he did,
backwards and in high heels.
Bob Thaves

• • • • •

In Hollywood, marriage is a success
if it outlives milk.
Rita Rudner

• • • • •

I married beneath me, all women do.
Nancy Astor

• • • • •

Twenty million women rose to their feet with
the cry "We will not be dictated to," and
promptly became stenographers.
G.K. Chesterton (on Women's Lib)

Brigands demand your money or your life;
women require both.
Samuel Butler

• • • • •

Men are like car alarms—they both make
a lot of noise no one listens to.
Diana Jordan

• • • • •

Another instance of the triumph of
hope over experience.
Samuel Johnson (of the remarriage
of a widowed friend)

• • • • •

Madam, don't you have any
unexpressed thoughts?
George S. Kaufman

• • • • •

Women are more irritable than men, probably
because men are more irritating.
Anon

When a man steals your wife, there is no better
revenge than to let him keep her.
Sacha Guitry

· · · · ·

The only way to get rid of cockroaches is to tell
them you want a long term relationship.
Jasmine Birtles

· · · · ·

Men forget everything;
women remember everything.
John Wayne

· · · · ·

Nobody will ever win the battle of the sexes.
There's too much fraternizing with the enemy.
Henry Kissinger

· · · · ·

The weaker sex are the stronger sex because of
the weakness of the stronger sex
for the weaker sex.
Anon

All men are of the same mold but some
are moldier than others.
Anon

• • • • •

A divorce costs much more than a wedding
but it's worth it.
Anon

• • • • •

Why should women mind if men have
their faces on the money as long as we
have our hands on it?
Ivy Priest

• • • • •

The hardest task in a girl's life is to prove to
a man that his intentions are serious.
Helen Rowland

• • • • •

you think women are the weaker sex, try pulling
the blankets back to your side.
Stuart Turner

We pondered whether to take a holiday or get a divorce, and we decided that a trip to Bermuda is over in two weeks, but a divorce is something you always have.
Woody Allen

• • • • •

Is it time for your medication or mine?
Anon

• • • • •

One of the most difficult things in this world is to convince a woman that even a bargain costs money.
Edgar Howe

• • • • •

Instead of getting married again, I'm going to find a woman I don't like and give her a house.
Lewis Grizzard

• • • • •

Macho does not prove mucho.
Zsa Zsa Gabor

And the judge said "All the money and we'll shorten it to alimony."
Robin Williams

• • • • •

The critical period in matrimony is breakfast time.
A.P. Herbert

• • • • •

At whatever stage you apologize to your wife, the answer is always the same: "It's too late now."
Denys Parsons

• • • • •

The feminine vanity case is the grave of masculine illusions.
Helen Rowland

• • • • •

A woman told me she would fulfill my ultimate fantasy for $100—so I asked her to paint my house.
Sean O'Bryan

English is called the mother tongue because father seldom gets a chance to use it.

Anon

• • • • •

Always suspect any job men willingly vacate for women.

Jill Tweedie

• • • • •

It isn't premarital sex if you have no intention of getting married.

Matt Barry

• • • • •

Give a man a free hand and he'll run it all over you.

Mae West

• • • • •

A good husband is one who will wash up when asked and dry up when told.

Anon

After a man is married he has the legal right
to deceive only one woman.
Edgar Howe

•••••

Divorce is the best way of getting rid
of a tiresome mother-in-law.
Anon

•••••

The female sex has no greater fan than I,
and I have the bills to prove it.
Alan Jay Lerner

•••••

A husband is what is left of a lover, after
the nerve has been extracted.
Helen Rowland

•••••

Never trust a husband too far,
nor a bachelor too near.
Helen Rowland

Chapter 4

That's Life

If you don't drink, smoke or drive a car,
you're a tax evader.
Tom Foley

Enjoy these scathing statements and philosophical asides concerning the comedy of human living: money, religion, sport, people and places (not without a smattering of xenophobia), food and drink, age, health, and death.

• • • • •

If you think nobody cares whether you are alive or dead, try missing a couple of car payments.
Ann Landers

• • • • •

It was one of those perfect summer days—the sun was shining, a breeze was blowing, the birds were singing, and the lawnmower was broken.
James Dent

• • • • •

How is it that the first piece of luggage on the airport carousel never belongs to anyone?
George Roberts

• • • • •

I'm not tense, just terribly, terribly alert.
Anon

Life is something to do when you
can't get to sleep.
Fran Lebowitz

• • • • •

You may know by my size that I have a
kind of alacrity in sinking.
Falstaff in Shakespeare's *The Merry Wives
of Windsor*

• • • • •

The consumer isn't a moron; she is your wife.
David Ogilvy

• • • • •

Hardware is the part of the computer
than can be kicked.
Jeff Pesis

• • • • •

Perennials are the ones that grow like weeds,
biennials are the ones that die this year
instead of next, and hardy annuals are
the ones that never come up at all.
Katharine Whitehorn

Never let the facts get in the way of a good story.
Anon

• • • • •

Sending men to that army is like
shoveling fleas across a barnyard—not
half of them get there.
Abraham Lincoln (of General McClellan's army)

• • • • •

Every man has the right to be conceited
until he is successful.
Benjamin Disraeli

• • • • •

A man described as a "sportsman" is generally a
bookmaker who takes actresses to night clubs.
Jimmy Cannon

• • • • •

A gossip is one who talks to you about other
people; a bore is one who talks about himself;
a brilliant conversationalist is one
who talks to you about yourself.
William King

Please don't ask me to relax—it's only the tension that's holding me together.
Helen Murray

• • • • •

I am determined to travel through life first class.
Noël Coward

• • • • •

Patience: a minor form of despair, disguised as a virtue.
Ambrose Bierce

• • • • •

A neurosis is a secret you don't know you're keeping.
Kenneth Tynan

• • • • •

If it squirms, it's biology; if it stinks, it's chemistry; if it doesn't work, it's physics, and if you can't understand it, it's mathematics.
Magnus Pyke

I'm trusting in the Lord and a good lawyer.
Oliver North

• • • • •

I have a previous engagement which
I will make as soon as possible.
John Barrymore (to an unwanted invitation)

• • • • •

Conscience is the inner voice which warns us
that somebody may be looking.
H.L. Mencken

• • • • •

History repeats itself;
historians repeat each other.
Philip Guedalla

• • • • •

They claim to be he-men, but the hair from
their combined chests wouldn't have
made a wig for a grape.
Robert Benchley

Seriousness is stupidity sent to college.
P.J. O'Rourke

• • • • •

Genius is one per cent inspiration,
ninety-nine per cent perspiration.
Thomas Alva Edison

• • • • •

Science is his forte, and omniscience his foible.
Sydney Smith (of William Whewell)

• • • • •

He listens to his psychiatrist, and then
draws his own confusions.
Anon

• • • • •

Keep a diary and some day it'll keep you.
Mae West

• • • • •

Assassination is the extreme form of censorship
George Bernard Shaw

Good people sleep better than bad people, but bad people enjoy the waking hours much more.
Woody Allen

• • • • •

I refuse to endure months of expensive humiliation only to be told that at the age of four I was in love with my rocking-horse.
Noël Coward

• • • • •

Early to bed and early to rise probably indicates unskilled labor.
John Ciardi

• • • • •

Several excuses are always less convincing than one.
Aldous Huxley

• • • • •

Excuse me, my leg has gone to sleep —do you mind if I join it?
Alexander Woollcott (to a person boring him at a party)

Luck is a matter of preparation
meeting opportunity.
Oprah Winfrey

• • • • •

He has impeccable bad taste.
Otis Ferguson

• • • • •

I never forget a face, but in your case I'll be glad
to make an exception.
Groucho Marx

• • • • •

Why do you sit there looking like an envelope
without any address on it?
Mark Twain

• • • • •

He never goes back on his word—without
consulting his lawyer.
Anon

He gets offended when others talk while he's interrupting.
Anon

• • • • •

Nothing is more responsible for the good old days than a bad memory.
Frank P. Adams

• • • • •

I do desire we may be better strangers.
William Shakespeare (from *As You Like It*)

• • • • •

He's a real big gun—of small caliber and immense bore.
Anon

• • • • •

If you're enjoying yourself in his company, it's all you're enjoying.
Anon

Haste is the mother of imperfection.
Anon

• • • • •

The aristocracy is composed chiefly of
asses—asses who talk about horses.
Heinrich Heine

• • • • •

Sweep on, you fat and greasy citizens.
William Shakespeare
(from *As You Like It*)

• • • • •

Money is not the only answer,
but it makes a difference.
Barack Obama

• • • • •

I don't know why she has such objections to birth
control; she's a living argument for it.
Anon

Life is divided into the horrible
and the miserable.
Woody Allen

• • • • •

It's surprising how such a big head holds
such a small brain.
Anon

• • • • •

You're a parasite for sore eyes.
Gregory Ratoff

• • • • •

My face looks like a wedding cake
left out in the rain.
W.H. Auden

• • • • •

Have some tongue, like cures like.
Robert Yelverton Tyrrell
(to a boring dining companion)

His egotism is a plain case of mistaken nonentity.
Anon

• • • • •

He lights up a room when he leaves it.
Anon

• • • • •

He has attained such a depth of seediness that
a flock of starlings could feed off him.
Clive James

• • • • •

When a bore leaves the room,
you feel as if someone came in.
Anon

• • • • •

Only dull people are brilliant at breakfast.
Oscar Wilde

• • • • •

Golf is a good walk spoiled.
Mark Twain

I used to think the only use for sport was to give small boys something else to kick besides me.
Katharine Whitehorn

• • • • •

Eamon D'Arcy has a golf swing like an octopus falling out of a tree.
David Feherty

• • • • •

The trouble with jogging is that by the time you realize you're not fit enough to do it, it's a long walk home.
Anon

• • • • •

The uglier a man's legs are, the better he plays golf—it's almost a law.
H.G. Wells

• • • • •

I always try to balance the light with the heavy—a few tears of human spirit in with the sequins and the fringes.
Bette Midler

If you think it's difficult to meet new people, try picking up the wrong golf ball.
Jack Lemmon

• • • • •

A little more moderation would be good; of course, my life hasn't exactly been one of moderation.
Donald Trump

• • • • •

Joggers are basically neurotic, bony, smug types who could bore the paint off a DC-10.
Rick Reilly

• • • • •

I do not participate in any sport that has ambulances at the bottom of the hill.
Erma Bombeck

• • • • •

Drama is life with the dull bits cut out.
Alfred Hitchcock

I don't think the discus will ever attract any interest until we start throwing them at each other.
Al Oerter

• • • • •

Reality: a delusion created by an alcohol deficiency.
Anon

• • • • •

I saw a notice which said "Drink Canada Dry" so I've started.
Brendan Behan

• • • • •

All I can say is that I have taken more out of alcohol than alcohol has taken out of me.
Winston Churchill

• • • • •

It's always hard to see hope with a hangover.
P.J. O'Rourke

A woman drove me to drink and I never even
had the courtesy to thank her.
W.C. Fields

• • • • •

But I'm not so think as you drunk I am.
J.C. Squire

• • • • •

A good rule is to state that the bouquet is better
than the taste, and vice versa.
Stephen Potter (on wine tasting)

• • • • •

You're not drunk if you can lie on the
floor without holding on.
Dean Martin

• • • • •

We drink to one another's healths,
and spoil our own.
Jerome K. Jerome

He goes into a bar optimistically and
comes out misty optically.
Anon

•••••

Work is the curse of the drinking classes.
Oscar Wilde

•••••

I'm only a beer teetotaller,
not a champagne teetotaller.
George Bernard Shaw

•••••

Let's get out of these wet clothes
and into a dry Martini.
Mae West

•••••

This was a good dinner enough, to be sure;
but it was not a dinner to ask a man to.
Samuel Johnson

I never drink water—look at the way it rusts pipes.
W.C. Fields

• • • • •

I always wake up at the crack of ice.
Joe E. Lewis

• • • • •

I go by tummy-time and I want my dinner.
Winston Churchill

• • • • •

Never serve oysters in a month that has
no paycheck in it.
P.J. O'Rourke

• • • • •

The cook was a good cook as cooks go;
and as good cooks go, she went.
Saki

• • • •

His favorite drink is the next one.
Anon

He climbed the ladder of success kissing
the feet of the one ahead of him and
kicking the head of the one behind.
Anon

• • • • •

He was dull in a new way, and that made
many people think him great.
Samuel Johnson (of Thomas Gray)

• • • • •

When Soloman said there was a time and a place
for everything, he had not encountered
the problem of parking an automobile.
Bob Edwards

• • • • •

However harmless a thing is, if the law forbids it
most people will think it wrong.
W. Somerset Maugham

• • • • •

Whom the gods wish to destroy
they first call promising.
Cyril Connolly

An expert is one who knows more and more
about less and less.
Anon

• • • • •

An uneasy conscience is a hair in the mouth.
Mark Twain

• • • • •

Success is the one unpardonable sin
against our fellows.
Ambrose Bierce

• • • • •

There's a big difference between free speech
and cheap talk.
Anon

• • • • •

Circumstances make man,
not man circumstances.
Mark Twain

A boss is a person who's early when you're late
and late when you're early.
Anon

· · · · ·

I think a grave has walked over this goose.
Noël Coward

· · · · ·

Existentialism means that no one else
can take a bath for you.
Delmore Schwartz

· · · · ·

We used to build civilizations;
now we build shopping malls.
Bill Bryson

· · · · ·

Not in doing what you like best, in liking what
you do is the secret of happiness.
J.M. Barrie

Envy is an admission of inferiority.
Victor Hugo

• • • • •

Anger makes dull men witty,
but it keeps them poor.
Francis Bacon

• • • • •

It is impossible to enjoy idling thoroughly
unless one has plenty of work to do.
Jerome K. Jerome

• • • • •

Calamities are of two kinds: misfortune to
ourselves, and good fortune to others.
Ambrose Bierce

• • • • •

Humor is emotional chaos
remembered in tranquility.
James Thurber

Everyone sits in the prison of his own ideas.
Albert Einstein

• • • • •

One of the most difficult things to give away
is kindness—it is usually returned.
Anon

• • • • •

If you want the last word in an argument say:
"I expect you're right."
Anon

• • • • •

You know what they say, if at first you don't
succeed, you're not the only son.
Stephen Fry

• • • • •

It was beautiful and simple as all
truly great swindles are.
O. Henry

If at first you don't succeed—you're fired.
Jen Graman

• • • • •

As one door closes, another slams in your face.
Rachel Heyhoe Flint

• • • • •

Nothing is impossible for people who don't have
to do it themselves.
Anon

• • • • •

On the day of victory, no fatigue is felt.
Arabic proverb

• • • • •

After you've heard two eyewitness accounts of an
accident, it makes you wonder about history.
Dave Barry

• • • • •

A committee is an animal with four back legs.
John Le Carré

A camel is a horse designed by a committee.
Alec Issigonis

• • • • •

A home keeps you from living with your parents.
P.J. O'Rourke

• • • • •

We ought never do wrong when
people are looking.
Mark Twain

• • • • •

Don't let yesterday take up too much of today.
Will Rogers

• • • • •

Absurdity: a statement of belief inconsistent
with one's own opinion.
Anon

• • • • •

A wit with dunces, and a dunce with wits.
Alexander Pope

There is sufficiency in the world for man's need but not for man's greed.
Mahatma Gandhi

• • • • •

Better to keep your mouth shut and appear stupid than to open it and remove all doubt.
Mark Twain

• • • • •

If you don't believe in the resurrection of the dead, look at any office at quitting time.
Robert Townsend

• • • • •

The impossible: something that nobody can do—until somebody does it.
Anon

• • • • •

Foolproof systems do not take into account the ingenuity of fools.
Gene Brown

Make three correct guesses consecutively and
everyone will regard you as an expert.
Anon

• • • • •

If you don't fail now and again,
it's a sign you're playing it safe.
Woody Allen

• • • • •

Blessed is he who, having nothing to say, abstains
from giving evidence of that fact.
George Eliot

• • • • •

The trouble with the rat-race is that even if
you win, you're still a rat.
Lily Tomlin

• • • • •

All you need to grow fine, vigorous grass is
a crack in your sidewalk.
James Hewett

The French don't care what they do as long as they pronounce it properly.
George Bernard Shaw

• • • • •

England and America are two countries divided by a common language.
George Bernard Shaw

• • • • •

The Irish are a fair people; they never speak well of one another.
Samuel Johnson

• • • • •

The best thing I know between France and England is—the sea.
Douglas Jerrold

• • • • •

California is a fine place to live—if you happen to be an orange.
Fred Allen

There's only one thing in the world worse than being talked about and that is not being talked about.
Oscar Wilde

• • • • •

Life happens too fast for you ever to think about it—you could just persuade people of this, but they insist on amassing information.
Kurt Vonnegut

• • • • •

There are only two types of exercise in Hollywood: jogging and helping a divorced friend move.
Robert Wagner

• • • • •

Fine art and pizza delivery: what we do falls neatly in between.
David Letterman

Canadians are Americans with no Disneyland.
Margaret Mahy

• • • • •

If ever there was an aviary overstocked with
jays it is that Yaptown-on-the-Hudson
called New York.
O. Henry

• • • • •

Norway—the sun never sets, the bar never opens,
and the whole country smells of kippers.
Evelyn Waugh

• • • • •

Americans love ice and hate cold water and so
the swimming pools are as hot as bouillabaisse.
Noël Coward

• • • • •

There are in England sixty different religious
sects and only one sauce.
Francesco Caracciolo

In India, "cold weather" is merely a conventional phrase and has come into use through the necessity of having some way to distinguish between weather which will melt a brass door knob and weather which only makes it mushy.
Mark Twain

• • • • •

American women expect to find in their husbands the perfection that English women only hope to find in their butlers.
W. Somerset Maugham

• • • • •

I once heard a Californian student in Heidelberg say, in one of his calmest moods, that he would rather decline two drinks than one German adjective.
Mark Twain

• • • • •

Belgium is a country invented by the British to annoy the French.
Charles de Gaulle

I know why the sun never sets on the British Empire: God wouldn't trust an Englishman in the dark.
Duncan Spaeth

• • • • •

You cannot underestimate the intelligence of the American people.
H.L. Mencken

• • • • •

The French are the masters of "the dog ate my homework" school of diplomatic relations.
P.J. O'Rourke

• • • • •

The perfidious, haughty, savage, disdainful, stupid, slothful, inhospitable, inhuman English.
Julius Caesar Scaliger

• • • • •

Wars and elections are both too big and too small to matter in the long run. The daily work—that goes on, it adds up.
Barbara Kingsolver

I still have my feet on the ground,
I just wear better shoes.
Oprah Winfrey

• • • • •

If someone says: "It's not the money, it's the
principle," it's the money.
Angelo Valenti

• • • • •

It's not that it is so good with money,
but that it's so bad without it.
Anon

• • • • •

Money makes money and the money money
makes makes money.
Benjamin Franklin

• • • • •

If economists were any good at business,
they would be rich men instead of
advisers to rich men.
Kirk Kerkorian

A bank is a place that will lend you money if you can prove that you don't need it.
Bob Hope

• • • • •

Life is like a ten-speed bicycle.
Most of us have gears we never use.
Charles Schulz

• • • • •

Prosperity is the best protector of principle.
Mark Twain

• • • • •

When a man tells you he got rich by hard work, just ask him whose.
Anon

• • • • •

The two most beautiful words in the English language are "Check Enclosed."
Dorothy Parker

Death is the most convenient time
to tax rich people.
David Lloyd George

• • • • •

Business conventions are important because
they demonstrate how many people a company
can operate without.
J.K. Galbraith

• • • • •

Where there's a will there are relations.
Michael Gill

• • • • •

Expenditure rises to meet income.
C. Northcote Parkinson

• • • • •

I started out with nothing
and I've still got most of it left.
Anon

Some people go to church only when they are
being baptized, married, or buried—hatched,
matched, and dispatched.
James Hewett

• • • • •

I am always most religious upon a sunshiny day.
Lord Byron

• • • • •

Thanks to God, I am still an atheist.
Luis Buñuel

• • • • •

He prays on his knees on Sunday and on
everybody the rest of the week.
Anon

• • • • •

It is no accident that the symbol of a bishop
is a crook and the symbol of an archbishop
is a doublecross.
Gregory Dix

God will pardon me, it is His trade.
Heinrich Heine

• • • • •

If God had meant us to walk around naked, he
would never have invented the wicker chair.
Erma Bombeck

• • • • •

It only rains straight down—God
doesn't do windows.
Steven Wright

• • • • •

God is not dead but alive and working on
a much less ambitious project.
Anon

• • • • •

A Christian is a man who feels repentance
on a Sunday for what he did on Saturday
and is going to do on Monday.
Thomas Ybarra

God is a man, so it must be all rot.
Nancy Nicholson

• • • • •

Baptists are only funny underwater.
Neil Simon

• • • • •

Maturity is a high price to pay for growing up.
Tom Stoppard

• • • • •

By the time a person gets to greener pastures,
he can't climb the fence.
Anon

• • • • •

Don't worry about senility—when it hits you,
you won't know it.
Bill Cosby

• • • • •

Either he's dead, or my watch has stopped.
Groucho Marx

Two things grow weaker with the
years—teeth and memory.
Anon

• • • • •

Excuse my dust.
Dorothy Parker (suggested epitaph)

• • • • •

To me old age is always fifteen years
older than I am.
Bernard Baruch

• • • • •

The report of my death was an exaggeration.
Mark Twain

• • • • •

Death is nature's way of telling you to slow down.
Anon

• • • • •

Here am I, dying of a hundred good symptoms.
Alexander Pope

Memorial services are the cocktail party
of the geriatric set.
Ralph Richardson

• • • • •

I'm at the age where my back goes out
more than I do.
Phyllis Diller

• • • • •

I got fired because of my age—I'll never make
the mistake of being seventy again.
Casey Stengel

• • • • •

Immortality is the condition of a dead man
who does not believe he is dead.
H.L. Mencken

• • • • •

As a teenager you are in the last stage of life
when you will be happy to hear
that the phone is for you.
Fran Lebowitz

Birth, life, and death—each took place on the hidden side of a leaf.
Toni Morrison

• • • • •

If I wanted to hear the pitter patter of tiny feet I'd put shoes on my cat.
Anon

• • • • •

Even when freshly washed and relieved of all obvious confections, children tend to be sticky.
Fran Lebowitz

• • • • •

The only advantage to being an adult is that you can eat your dessert without having eaten your vegetables.
Lisa Alther

• • • • •

Money isn't everything, but it sure keeps you in touch with your children.
J. Paul Getty

To be a successful father, there's one absolute rule: when you have a kid, don't look at it for the first two years.
Ernest Hemingway

• • • • •

It is not advisable to put your head around your child's door to see if it is asleep—it was.
Faith Hines

• • • • •

My mother loved children—she would have given anything if I had been one.
Groucho Marx

• • • • •

Telling a teenager the facts of life is like giving a fish a bath.
Arnold Glasow

• • • • •

Parents are the very last people who should be allowed to have children.
Anon

Children despise their parents until the age of forty, when they suddenly become just like them, thus preserving the system.
Quentin Crewe

• • • • •

Ask your child what he wants for dinner only if he's buying.
Fran Lebowitz

• • • • •

Some parents have difficulty deciding on a name for the new baby, but others have rich relatives.
Don McElroy

• • • • •

I don't believe in smacking children—I just use a cattle prod.
Jenny Eclair

• • • • •

Perhaps host and guest is really the happiest relation for father and son.
Evelyn Waugh

Always obey your parents, when they are present.
Mark Twain

• • • • •

She's aged more than her husband,
but less often.
Anon

• • • • •

Some extraordinarily unlikely women do have it.
Noël Coward (on sex appeal)

• • • • •

The "g" is silent—the only part of her that is.
Julie Burchill (of Camille Paglia)

• • • • •

When women go wrong, men go right after them
Mae West

• • • • •

She wears too much of not enough.
Anon

I don't like to share my personal life...it wouldn't
be personal if I shared it.
George Clooney

• • • • •

Her once dangerous curves have become
extended detours.
Anon

• • • • •

Show me a woman who doesn't feel guilt
and I'll show you a man.
Erica Jong

• • • • •

Women give themselves to God when the devil
wants nothing more from them.
Sophie Arnould

• • • • •

If that's mink she's wearing,
some rabbit must be living under
an assumed name.
Anon

A woman without a man is like a fish
without a bicycle.
Gloria Steinem (attrib.)

• • • • •

The best years of her life were the ten between
twenty-nine and thirty.
Anon

• • • • •

She wears the kind of dresses that
start late and end early.
Anon

• • • • •

A man without a woman is like a moose
without a hat-rack.
Arthur Marshall

• • • • •

Outside every thin girl there's a fat man
trying to get in.
Katherine Whitehorn

She finally admitted she was forty,
but she didn't say when.
Anon

• • • • •

I refuse to admit that I'm more than fifty-two,
even if that does make my sons illegitimate.
Nancy Astor

• • • • •

She dresses for the nuclear age—with
fifty percent fall out.
Anon

• • • • •

She's not what she was fifteen years ago—she's
nine years older.
Anon

• • • • •

She wears the kind of bikini that's based on the
theory that nothing succeeds like nothing.
Anon

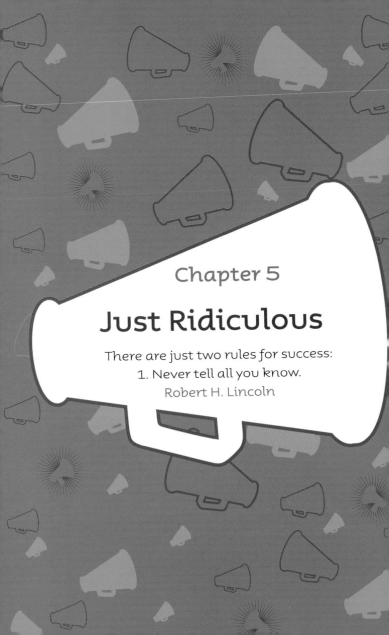

Chapter 5

Just Ridiculous

There are just two rules for success:
1. Never tell all you know.
Robert H. Lincoln

A collection of bizarre sayings—the things we find funny without really knowing why, as well as some "foot in mouth" comments which their authors will have wished they hadn't said.

• • • • •

The Moon may be smaller than the Earth, but it's farther away.
Steven Wright

• • • • •

If you get to be one hundred you've got it made—very few people die past that age.
George Burns

• • • • •

I could see that, if not actually disgruntled, he was far from gruntled.
P.G. Wodehouse

• • • • •

Most people who are as attractive, witty, and intelligent as I am are usually conceited.
Joan Rivers

The Venus de Milo is a good example of
what happens to somebody who won't
stop biting her fingernails.
Will Rogers

• • • • •

I used to think that the human brain was
the most fascinating part of the body and
then I realized, "What is telling me that?"
Emo Phillips

• • • • •

'I digress,' as the bride said when she got up in the
middle of the night and baked a cake.
Noël Coward

• • • • •

Passionate hatred can give meaning and purpose
to an empty life.
Eric Hoffer

• • • • •

A bore: someone who talks when you
want him to listen.
Ambrose Bierce

I told my psychiatrist that everyone hates me. He said I was being ridiculous—everyone hasn't met me yet.
Rodney Dangerfield

• • • • •

I'm not bald—my head is just a solar panel for a sex machine.
Telly Savalas

• • • • •

If the garbage man calls, tell him we don't want any.
Groucho Marx

• • • • •

I don't go to my psychiatrist any more—he was meddling too much in my private life.
Anon

• • • • •

Dolphins are so intelligent that within only a few weeks they can train a man to throw fish at them from the side of a pool.
Anon

Old MacDonald was dyslexic, IEIEO.
Billy Connolly

• • • • •

What's another word for Thesaurus?
Anon

• • • • •

I have a fine sense of the ridiculous,
but no sense of humor.
Edward Albee

• • • • •

Reality is for people who can't face drugs.
Laurence Peter

• • • • •

All you need is love, but a little chocolate
now and then doesn't hurt.
Charles Schulz

• • • • •

Policemen, like red squirrels, must be protected.
Joe Orton

Anybody who isn't pulling his weight is probably pushing his luck.
Anon

• • • • •

One of us must go.
Oscar Wilde (of the wallpaper which he could see from his deathbed)

• • • • •

I would have killed myself but my analyst was a strict Freudian and if you kill yourself they make you pay for the sessions you miss.
Woody Allen

• • • • •

Always end the name of your child with a vowel, so that when you yell the name will carry.
Bill Cosby

• • • • •

Everywhere is within walking distance if you have the time.
Steven Wright

First things first, second things never.
Shirley Conran

• • • • •

I always wanted to be somebody, but now I realize
I should have been more specific.
Lily Tomlin

• • • • •

I learned law so well, the day I graduated I sued
the college and got my tuition fees back.
Fred Allen

• • • • •

He that but looketh on a plate of ham and eggs to
lust after it, hath already committed
breakfast with it in his heart.
C.S. Lewis

• • • • •

Ignorance of the law must not prevent the losing
lawyer from collecting his fee.
John Mortimer

Human beings are the only creatures
on earth that allow their children
to come back home.
Bill Cosby

• • • • •

Eyewitnesses were on the scene in minutes.
Adam Boulton

• • • • •

Recreations: growling, prowling,
scowling, and owling.
Nicholas Fairbairn's entry in *Who's Who*

• • • • •

Coincide: what you do when it starts raining.
Anon

• • • • •

The insurance man told me that I was
covered for falling off the roof
but not for hitting the ground.
Tommy Cooper

Does the name Pavlov ring a bell?
Anon

• • • • •

There's a fine line between fishing and standing
on the riverside looking like an idiot.
Anon

• • • • •

People always ask me, "Were you funny as a
child?" Well, no, I was an accountant.
Ellen DeGeneres

• • • • •

The quickest way to make a red light
turn green is to try to find something in
the glove compartment.
Gary Doney

• • • • •

I love flying—I've been to almost as many
places as my luggage.
Bob Hope

I'm writing an unauthorized autobiography.
Steven Wright

• • • • •

Cross-country skiing is great if you live
in a small country.
Anon

• • • • •

Any man who grows to be more than five feet
seven inches is a weed.
Frank Lloyd Wright

• • • • •

After twelve years of therapy my psychiatrist said
something that brought tears to my eyes—he
said, "No hablo ingles."
Ronnie Shakes

• • • • •

I installed a skylight in my apartment and the
people who live above me are furious!
Steven Wright

George Burns is old enough to be his father.
Red Buttons

• • • • •

There aren't enough days in the weekend.
Anon

• • • • •

My theory of evolution is that
Darwin was adopted.
Steven Wright

• • • • •

A lot of people never use their initiative because
nobody ever tells them to.
Mary Allen

• • • • •

Smoking will cure weight problems . . . eventually.
Anon

• • • • •

The key to tennis is to win the last point.
Jim Courier

If in the last few years you haven't discarded a major opinion or acquired a new one, check your pulse—you may be dead.

Anon

• • • • •

I took a course in speed waiting—now I can wait an hour in only ten minutes.

Steven Wright

• • • • •

Have you heard the one about the nudist who plays strip poker—every time he loses, he has to put something on.

Anon

• • • • •

Just when you think tomorrow will never come, it's yesterday.

Anon

• • • • •

...side from its purchasing power, money is useless as far as I'm concerned.

Alfred Hitchcock

Is "tired old cliché" one?
Steven Wright

• • • • •

Give me a smart idiot before a
stupid genius any day.
Samuel Goldwyn

• • • • •

What's wrong with being a boring kind of guy?
George Bush

• • • • •

I love California—I practically grew up in Phoenix.
Dan Quayle

• • • • •

Bambi—see the movie! Eat the cast!
Henry Kelly

• • • • •

If we don't succeed, we run the risk of failure.
Dan Quayle

I would have given my right arm to
have been a pianist.
Bobby Robson

* * * * *

One word sums up the responsibility of any
Vice-President, and that word is "to be prepared."
Dan Quayle

* * * * *

A lot of people my age are dead
at the present time.
Casey Stengel

* * * * *

Did you get a good look at my face
when I took your purse?
Accused thief who undertook
his own defense (and lost)

* * * * *

A lot of horses get distracted—it's
just human nature.
Nick Zito

Anything that man says you've got to take
with a dose of salts.
Samuel Goldwyn

• • • • •

When it comes to ruining a painting,
he's an artist.
Samuel Goldwyn

• • • • •

He'll regret it to his dying day,
if ever he lives that long.
Frank Nugent

• • • • •

I got up more nostrils than there are noses.
Andrew Neil

• • • • •

Jim Morrison is dead now and that's a high
price to pay for immortality.
Gloria Estefan

Food is an important part
of a balanced diet.
Fran Lebowitz

• • • • •

There's always a choice of whether one does it
last week, this week, or next week.
John Major

• • • • •

Ve are going to have the best educated American
people in the world.
Dan Quayle

• • • •

I'm for a stronger death penalty.
George Bush

• • • • •

Anyone who goes to see a psychiatrist ought
to have his head examined.
Samuel Goldwyn

I want to make sure that everyone who
has a job wants a job.
George Bush

● ● ● ● ●

I read part of it all the way through.
Samuel Goldwyn

● ● ● ● ●

We are not ready for any unforeseen event
that may or may not occur.
Dan Quayle

● ● ● ● ●

I am the literary equivalent of
a Big Mac and Fries.
Stephen King

● ● ● ● ●

The United States has much to offer
the Third World War.
Ronald Reagan (the mistake was
repeated nine times in one speech)

He's running a high temperature and his chest
looks like a bad Matisse.
Noël Coward (of a friend with chickenpox)

• • • • •

Dear 338171, May I call you 338?
Noël Coward's wartime letter to Lawrence of
Arabia (Aircraftsman T.E. Shaw, No. 338171)

• • • • •

Poets have been mysteriously silent
on the subject of cheese.
G.K. Chesterton

• • • • •

When the guy who made the first drawing board
got it wrong, what did he go back to?
Steven Wright

• • • • •

The trouble with this business is the
dearth of bad pictures.
Samuel Goldwyn

A friend is someone who will help you move;
a good friend is someone who will
help you move a body.
Alexei Sayle

• • • • •

A moose is an animal with horns on the
front of his head and a hunting lodge
wall on the back of it.
Groucho Marx

• • • • •

Once, during Prohibition, I was forced to live for
days on nothing but food and water.
W.C. Fields

• • • • •

Go and sing to them when the guns
are firing—that's your job!
Winston Churchill (to Noël Coward)

• • • • •

Alcoholic: a man you don't like who drinks
as much as you do.
Dylan Thomas

Light pranks add zest to your services,
but don't pull the customers' ears.
Rules for hotel chambermaids,
Japanese Tourist Board

• • • • •

I called my landlord and told him that my
apartment had terrible acoustics and he told me
he'd caught them all long before I moved in.
Anon

• • • • •

A cucumber should be well sliced, and dressed
with pepper and vinegar, and then thrown out,
as good for nothing.
Samuel Johnson

• • • • •

Nobody would wear beige to rob a bank.
Mickey Rose

• • • • •

A man could not be in two places at the same
time unless he were a bird.
Sir Boyle Roche

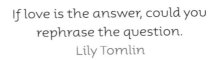

If love is the answer, could you
rephrase the question.
Lily Tomlin

•••••

Make-or-break situations, such as we have seen
here, can sometimes make as well as break.
Robin Oakley

•••••

Television is for appearing on, not looking at.
Noël Coward

•••••

Right now, I'm having amnesia and déjà vu at the
same time. I think I've forgotten this before.
Steven Wright

•••••

Gossip: hearing something you like about
someone you don't.
Earl Wilson

I'm giving you the chance to redeem your
character, something you have irretrievably lost.
Serjeant Arabin QC

• • • • •

I have my faults, but being wrong
isn't one of them.
Jimmy Hoffa

• • • • •

They pushed their nomination down my
throat behind my back.
J. Ramsay MacDonald

• • • • •

When I want your opinion, I'll give it to you.
Samuel Goldwyn

• • • • •

I wear very simple shoes—it is not one
of my weaknesses.
Imelda Marcos

Every Tom, Dick, and Harry is called Arthur.
Samuel Goldwyn

• • • • •

The single, overwhelming two facts were . . .
Paddy Ashdown

• • • • •

What's the plural of "ignited?"
Gaby Roslin

• • • • •

This is the worst disaster since I was elected.
Governor Pat Brown

• • • • •

I'll give it to you in two words: im possible.
Samuel Goldwyn

• • • • •

I can't see who's in the lead but it's either
Oxford or Cambridge.
John Snagge (commentating on
the 1949 Boat Race)

Researchers have already cast much darkness
on this subject and if they continue their
investigations we shall soon know
nothing at all about it.
Mark Twain

• • • • •

The trouble with referees is that they just
don't care which side wins.
Tom Canterbury

• • • • •

A verbal contract isn't worth the paper
it is written on.
Samuel Goldwyn

• • • • •

Why is the alphabet in that order—is it
because of that song?
Steven Wright

• • • • •

The doctors X-rayed my head
and found nothing.
Dizzy Dean

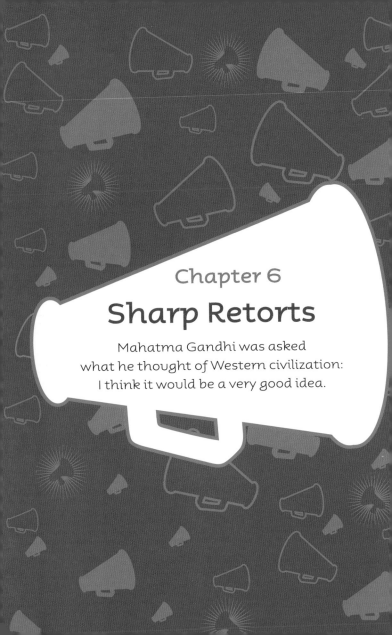

Chapter 6

Sharp Retorts

Mahatma Gandhi was asked
what he thought of Western civilization:
I think it would be a very good idea.

Our collection of one liners concludes with some snappy reposts from (mostly) the rich and famous which need a little explanation to put them in context.

• • • • •

When Senator Wyche Fowler was asked whether he had ever smoked marijuana, he replied: Only when committing adultery.

• • • • •

Churchill was sent two tickets to the opening of George Bernard Shaw's new play with the message: Bring a friend—if you have one. Churchill replied that he was otherwise engaged but would like to see the play's second performance: If there is one.

• • • • •

Calvin Coolidge, not known for his verbosity, was approached by a woman at a public function: Mr President, I have made a bet with my friends that I can make you say at least three words to me during dinner. You lose, came the reply.

During a concert one evening, Frank Zappa was dismayed to hear someone in the audience shout out, "Eat me, Zappa!" "Here I stand," Zappa replied, "hoping against hope that it's a chick with a low voice."

• • • • •

Asked if he and his wife, Vita Sackville-West, had ever collaborated on anything, Harold Nicolson replied: Yes, we have two sons.

• • • • •

When asked whether it was always sunny in Jamaica, Noël Coward answered:
Never at night.

• • • • •

Arguing against the necessity for a nation to be multilingual, Ralph Melnyk stated:
English was good enough for Jesus Christ.

• • • • •

When asked in an interview how his autobiography was progressing, Noël Coward replied:
Absolutely limping.

Joe Frazier (about Muhammad Ali): He's phony, using his blackness to get his way.
Muhammad Ali: Joe Frazier is so ugly he should donate his face to the US Bureau of Wildlife.

• • • • •

While in Egypt, T.E. Lawrence (Lawrence of Arabia) reluctantly attended a party hosted by a rather faded socialite who was famous for trying to befriend celebrities. Using the unseasonably hot weather as an opening, she sailed up to Lawrence saying: 92 today Colonel Lawrence! Imagine it! 92 today! Many happy returns, madam, Lawrence replied.

• • • • •

Thomas Beecham heard that Malcolm Sargent, whose nickname was "Flash Harry," was conducting concerts in Japan. He commented: Ah—Flash in Japan!

• • • • •

Singer: You know, I insured my voice for fifty thousand dollars.
Conductor: Really, and what did you do with the money?

When asked if he believed in God,
Noël Coward answered:
We've never been intimate.

• • • • •

On his deathbed, Voltaire was urged by a priest to
renounce the devil. He protested:
This is no time for making new enemies.

• • • • •

Asked why he had made a commercial for
American Express, Peter Ustinov answered:
To pay for my American Express.

• • • • •

As the playing of the orchestra began to
improve, Thomas Beecham commented
to violinist Jean Pougnet:
Don't look now, M. Pougnet, but I think
we're being followed.

• • • • •

The jazz musician, Zoot Sims, was asked how he
could play so well when he was loaded.
I practice when I'm loaded.

When a waiter spilled soup on her dress,
Beatrice Lillie complained:
Never darken my Dior again.

• • • • •

Groucho Marx was asked if Groucho was
his real name. He replied:
No, I'm breaking it in for a friend.

• • • • •

Noël Coward to Edna Ferber, who was wearing a
tailored suit: "You look almost like a man."
Edna Ferber: "So do you."

• • • • •

Did you mail that check to the judge?
Lawyer Roy M. Cohn (in public, to his assistant)

• • • • •

Arnold Toynbee, author of A Study of History,
which took him thirty-five years to complete,
was asked by a journalist what had impelled
him to devote that amount of time to a
single work. Curiosity.

Noël Coward was with a group of friends when someone announced that a boorish and overbearing acquaintance had "blown his brains out," to which Coward retorted: He must have been an incredibly good shot.

• • • • •

When John McCain first ran for election in Arizona, he was accused by his opponents of being a carpetbagger. His reply? While he would love to have spent more time in Arizona (as his rivals had), serving his country as an air force pilot and growing up as the son of a senior naval officer had both entailed moving—and living—all over the world. Indeed, the longest he had ever lived in any single place, he explained, was about five years...as a prisoner of war in Hanoi, Vietnam

• • • • •

George S. Kaufman, drama editor of the New York Times, was asked by an agent how they could get their leading actress's name into his newspaper. He replied: Shoot her.

During a speech, President William Howard Taft complained that there was so much noise in the audience he could hardly hear himself talk, to which someone at the back replied:
It's OK, you're not missing anything.

• • • • •

Tallulah Bankhead was asked by a male journalist if she had ever been mistaken for a man. Her reply: No, darling, have you?

• • • • •

Rejection slip for a poem entitled "Why Do I Live?"
Because you send your poem by mail.
Eugene Field

• • • • •

An actress, worried about ageing, confided to a friend that she dreaded the thought of forty-five. The "friend" asked: Why, what happened then?

Some crushing put-downs:

● ● ● ● ●

I enjoyed your book, who wrote it for you?
Darling, I'm so glad you liked it. Who read
it to you?

● ● ● ● ●

How about coming back to my place?
Will two people fit under a rock?

● ● ● ● ●

Hey, gorgeous, would you like a good time?
Sorry, I don't date outside my species.

● ● ● ● ●

How do you like your eggs in the morning?
Unfertilized.

● ● ● ● ●

No woman ever made a fool of me.
Who did then?

I didn't say it was your fault,
I said I was going to blame you.

● ● ● ● ●

It may be that your sole purpose
in life is simply to serve
as a warning to others.

● ● ● ● ●

You are depriving some poor village of its idiot.

● ● ● ● ●

Haven't I seen you someplace before?
Yeah, that's why I don't go there anymore.

● ● ● ● ●

Your place or mine?
Both. You go to yours and I'll go to mine.

● ● ● ● ●

I know how to please a woman.
Then please leave me alone.

Performers' responses to hecklers and some classic Shakespearean insults:

• • • • •

Look, this is my job—I don't turn up at your work and spit on the burgers.

• • • • •

Let me guess—tonight's square dance was canceled, right?

• • • • •

Thou whoreson zed! Thou unneccessary letter!
William Shakespeare

• • • • •

Peace, ye fat guts.
William Shakespeare

• • • • •

Away, thou issue of a mangy dog!
William Shakespeare

NOTES

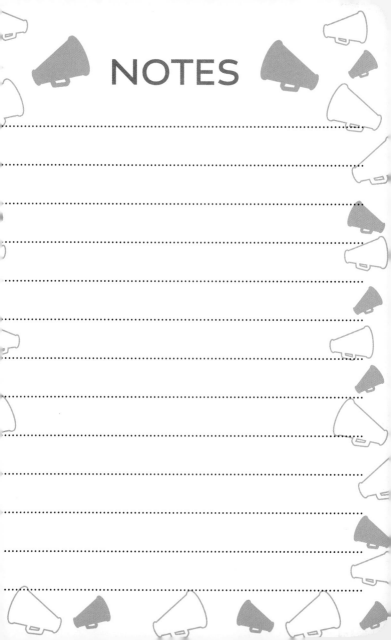

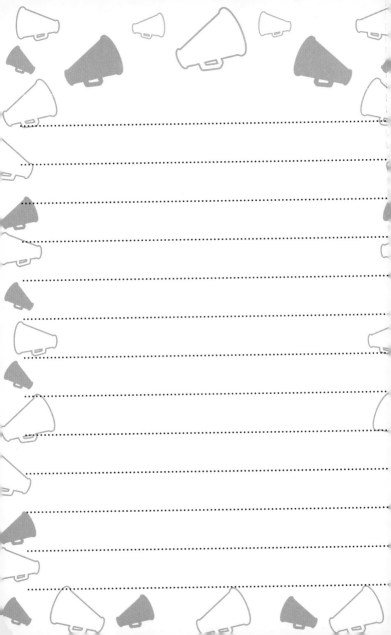

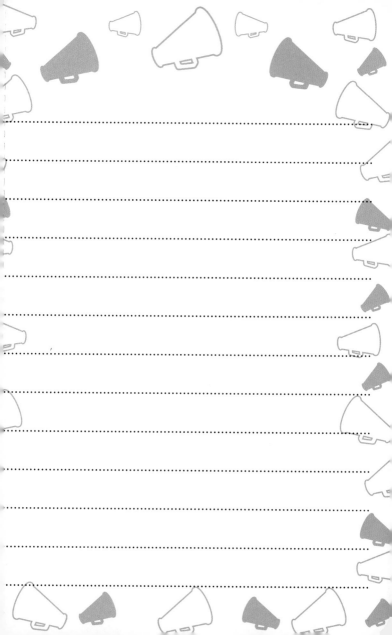

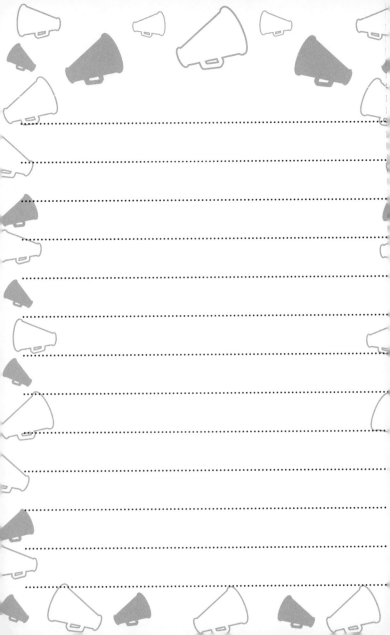

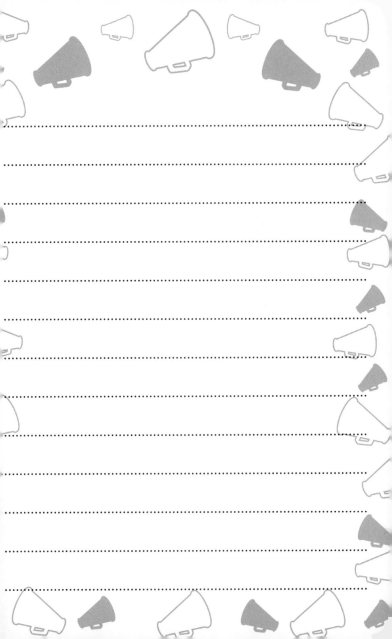

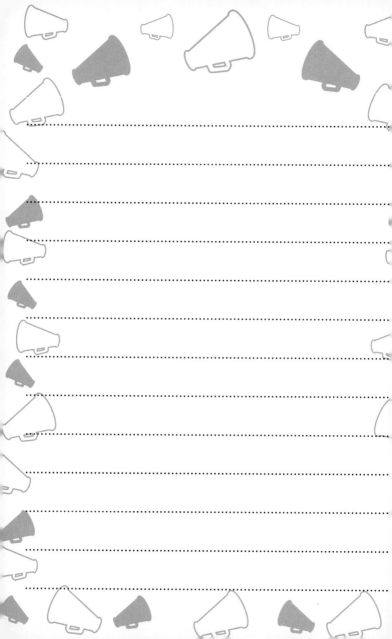

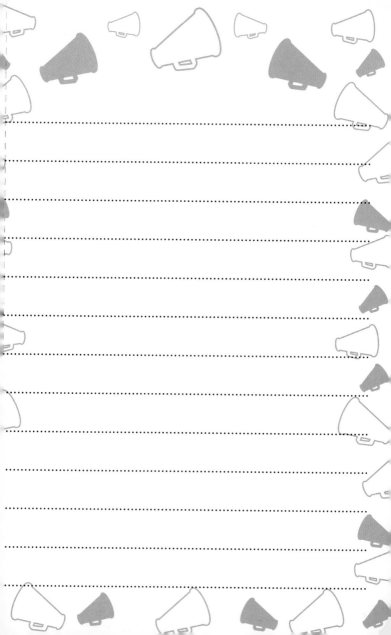

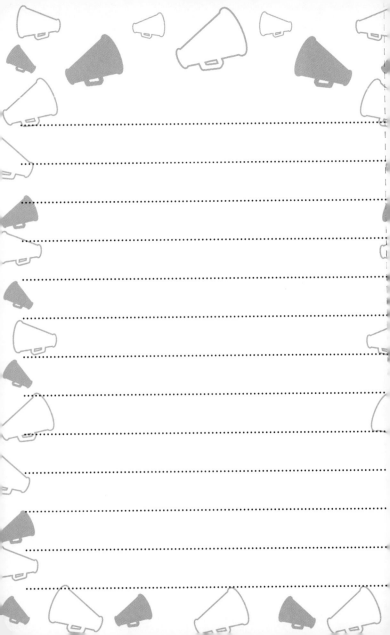

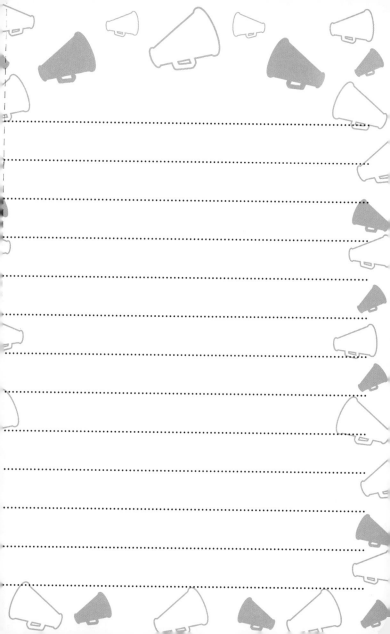

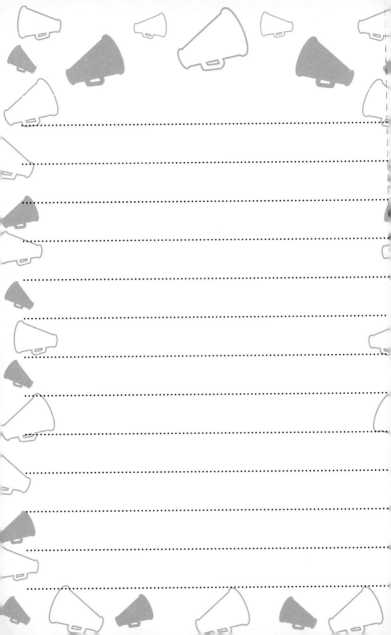

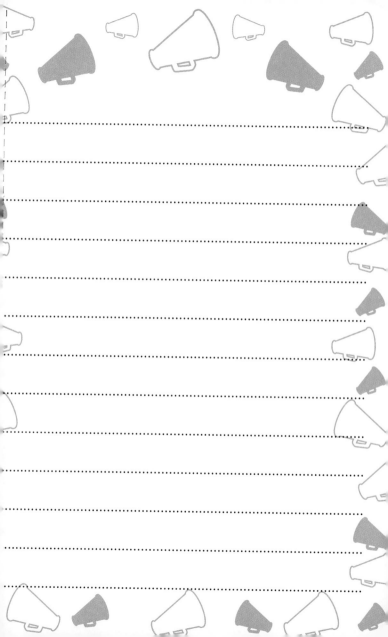

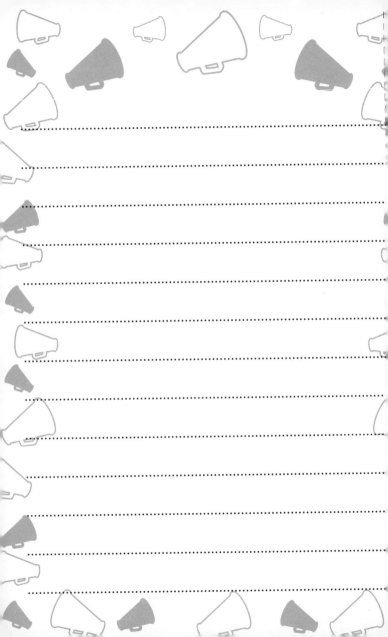

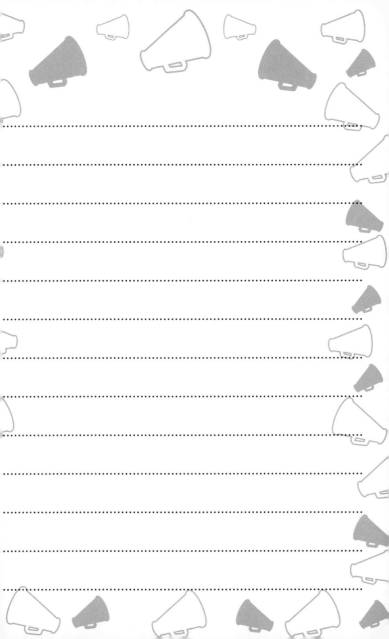

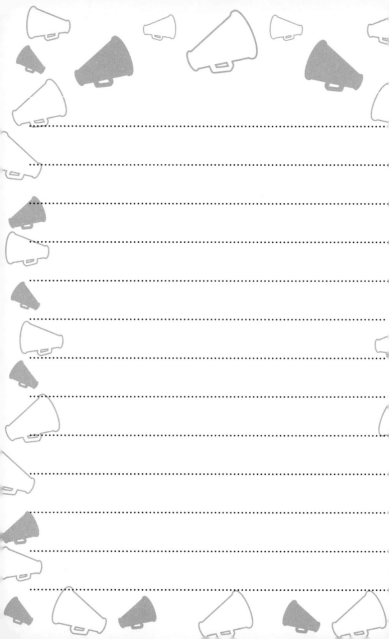

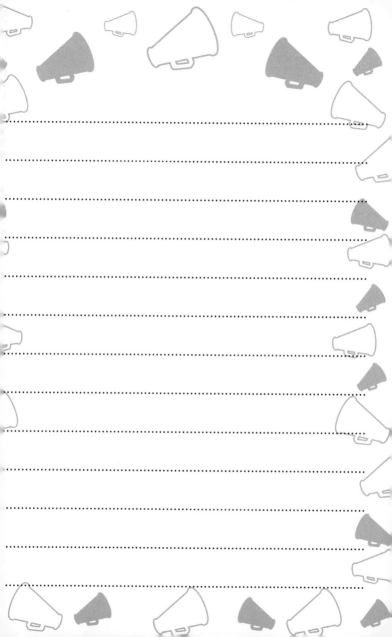

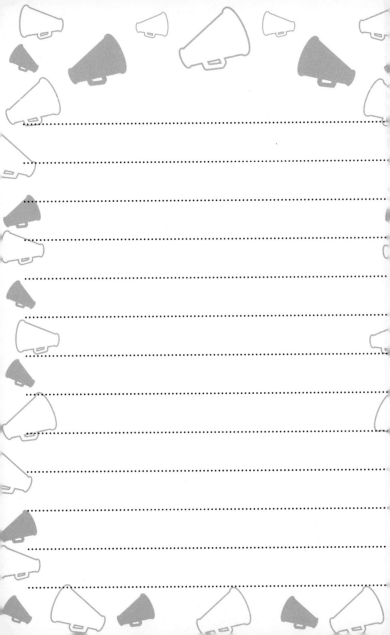